This Coaster Log Belongs To

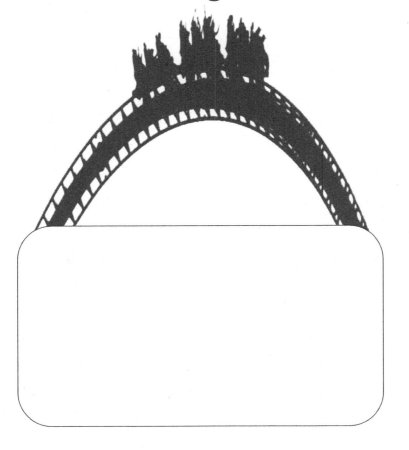

Roller Coaster Log

Date _____

Coaster Name _____

Location _____

Material: Steel or Wood   Year Opened _____

Designer _____

Type: Sit Down, Suspended, Wing, Flying,
       Stand Up, Bobsled, Pipeline

Thrill Level: 😒 😃 😳 🤯 😱

Height _____   Length _____

Speed _____   # of Inversions _____

Position: Front, Middle, Back

More About My Ride:

Roller Coaster Log

Date _____

Coaster Name _____

Location _____

Material: Steel or Wood   Year Opened _____

Designer _____

Type: Sit Down, Suspended, Wing, Flying,
          Stand Up, Bobsled, Pipeline

Thrill Level: 😌 😃 😳 🤯 😱

Height _____   Length _____

Speed _____   # of Inversions _____

Position: Front, Middle, Back

More About My Ride:

Roller Coaster Log

Date _____

Coaster Name _____

Location _____

Material: Steel or Wood   Year Opened _____

Designer _____

Type: Sit Down, Suspended, Wing, Flying,
       Stand Up, Bobsled, Pipeline

Thrill Level: 😏 😃 😳 😲 😱

Height _____   Length _____

Speed _____   # of Inversions _____

Position: Front, Middle, Back

More About My Ride:

Roller Coaster Log

Date _____

Coaster Name _____

Location _____

Material: Steel or Wood   Year Opened _____

Designer _____

Type: Sit Down, Suspended, Wing, Flying,
        Stand Up, Bobsled, Pipeline

Thrill Level: 😏 😃 😳 😵 😨

Height _____   Length _____

Speed _____   # of Inversions _____

Position: Front, Middle, Back

More About My Ride:

Roller Coaster Log

Date _____

Coaster Name _____

Location _____

Material: Steel or Wood   Year Opened _____

Designer _____

Type: Sit Down, Suspended, Wing, Flying,
        Stand Up, Bobsled, Pipeline

Thrill Level: 😌 😃 😳 🤯 😱

Height _____   Length _____

Speed _____   # of Inversions _____

Position: Front, Middle, Back

More About My Ride:

Roller Coaster Log

Date _____

Coaster Name _____

Location _____

Material: Steel or Wood   Year Opened _____

Designer _____

Type: Sit Down, Suspended, Wing, Flying,
      Stand Up, Bobsled, Pipeline

Thrill Level: 😏 😃 😳 🤯 ☺

Height _____   Length _____

Speed _____   # of Inversions _____

Position: Front, Middle, Back

More About My Ride:

Roller Coaster Log

Date _____

Coaster Name _____

Location _____

Material: Steel or Wood   Year Opened _____

Designer _____

Type: Sit Down, Suspended, Wing, Flying,
        Stand Up, Bobsled, Pipeline

Thrill Level: 😴   😃   😮   🤯   😱

Height _____   Length _____

Speed _____   # of Inversions _____

Position: Front, Middle, Back

More About My Ride:

Roller Coaster Log

Date _____

Coaster Name _____

Location _____

Material: Steel or Wood   Year Opened _____

Designer _____

Type: Sit Down, Suspended, Wing, Flying,
      Stand Up, Bobsled, Pipeline

Thrill Level: 😏 😃 😳 😱 😨

Height _____   Length _____

Speed _____   # of Inversions _____

Position: Front, Middle, Back

More About My Ride:

Roller Coaster Log

Date _____

Coaster Name _____

Location _____

Material: Steel or Wood   Year Opened _____

Designer _____

Type: Sit Down, Suspended, Wing, Flying,
       Stand Up, Bobsled, Pipeline

Thrill Level: 😒 😃 😯 😲 😱

Height _____   Length _____

Speed _____   # of Inversions _____

Position: Front, Middle, Back

More About My Ride:

Roller Coaster Log

Date _____

Coaster Name _____

Location _____

Material: Steel or Wood   Year Opened _____

Designer _____

Type: Sit Down, Suspended, Wing, Flying,
      Stand Up, Bobsled, Pipeline

Thrill Level: 😏 😃 😳 🤯 😱

Height _____   Length _____

Speed _____   # of Inversions _____

Position: Front, Middle, Back

More About My Ride:

Roller Coaster Log

Date _____

Coaster Name _____

Location _____

Material: Steel or Wood   Year Opened _____

Designer _____

Type: Sit Down, Suspended, Wing, Flying,
        Stand Up, Bobsled, Pipeline

Thrill Level: 😒 😃 😳 😱 😨

Height _____   Length _____

Speed _____   # of Inversions _____

Position: Front, Middle, Back

More About My Ride:

Roller Coaster Log

Date _____

Coaster Name _____

Location _____

Material: Steel or Wood   Year Opened _____

Designer _____

Type: Sit Down, Suspended, Wing, Flying,
       Stand Up, Bobsled, Pipeline

Thrill Level: 😌 😀 😮 🤯 😱

Height _____   Length _____

Speed _____   # of Inversions _____

Position: Front, Middle, Back

More About My Ride:

Roller Coaster Log

Date _____

Coaster Name _____

Location _____

Material: Steel or Wood   Year Opened _____

Designer _____

Type: Sit Down, Suspended, Wing, Flying,
       Stand Up, Bobsled, Pipeline

Thrill Level: 😒 😃 😳 🤯 😱

Height _____   Length _____

Speed _____   # of Inversions _____

Position: Front, Middle, Back

More About My Ride:

Roller Coaster Log

Date _____

Coaster Name _____

Location _____

Material: Steel or Wood   Year Opened _____

Designer _____

Type: Sit Down, Suspended, Wing, Flying,
      Stand Up, Bobsled, Pipeline

Thrill Level: 😌 😃 😯 😱 😨

Height _____   Length _____

Speed _____   # of Inversions _____

Position: Front, Middle, Back

More About My Ride:

Roller Coaster Log

Date _____

Coaster Name _____

Location _____

Material: Steel or Wood   Year Opened _____

Designer _____

Type: Sit Down, Suspended, Wing, Flying,
        Stand Up, Bobsled, Pipeline

Thrill Level: 😏 😃 😲 🤯 😱

Height _____   Length _____

Speed _____   # of Inversions _____

Position: Front, Middle, Back

More About My Ride:

Roller Coaster Log

Date _____

Coaster Name _____

Location _____

Material: Steel or Wood   Year Opened _____

Designer _____

Type: Sit Down, Suspended, Wing, Flying,
      Stand Up, Bobsled, Pipeline

Thrill Level: 😏 😃 😳 😵 😱

Height _____   Length _____

Speed _____   # of Inversions _____

Position: Front, Middle, Back

More About My Ride:

Roller Coaster Log

Date _____

Coaster Name _____

Location _____

Material: Steel or Wood   Year Opened _____

Designer _____

Type: Sit Down, Suspended, Wing, Flying,
        Stand Up, Bobsled, Pipeline

Thrill Level: 😔 😃 😳 😵 😱

Height _____   Length _____

Speed _____   # of Inversions _____

Position: Front, Middle, Back

More About My Ride:

Roller Coaster Log

Date _____

Coaster Name _____

Location _____

Material: Steel or Wood   Year Opened _____

Designer _____

Type: Sit Down, Suspended, Wing, Flying,
        Stand Up, Bobsled, Pipeline

Thrill Level: 😒 😀 😳 🤯 😱

Height _____   Length _____

Speed _____   # of Inversions _____

Position: Front, Middle, Back

More About My Ride:

Roller Coaster Log

Date _____

Coaster Name _____

Location _____

Material: Steel or Wood   Year Opened _____

Designer _____

Type: Sit Down, Suspended, Wing, Flying,
      Stand Up, Bobsled, Pipeline

Thrill Level: 😒 😃 😳 🤯 😱

Height _____   Length _____

Speed _____   # of Inversions _____

Position: Front, Middle, Back

More About My Ride:

Roller Coaster Log

Date _____

Coaster Name _____

Location _____

Material: Steel or Wood   Year Opened _____

Designer _____

Type: Sit Down, Suspended, Wing, Flying,
          Stand Up, Bobsled, Pipeline

Thrill Level: 😌 😃 😳 😲 😱

Height _____   Length _____

Speed _____   # of Inversions _____

Position: Front, Middle, Back

More About My Ride:

Roller Coaster Log

Date _____

Coaster Name _____

Location _____

Material: Steel or Wood   Year Opened _____

Designer _____

Type: Sit Down, Suspended, Wing, Flying,
      Stand Up, Bobsled, Pipeline

Thrill Level: 😏 😃 😳 😱 🤐

Height _____   Length _____

Speed _____   # of Inversions _____

Position: Front, Middle, Back

More About My Ride:

Roller Coaster Log

Date _____

Coaster Name _____

Location _____

Material: Steel or Wood   Year Opened _____

Designer _____

Type: Sit Down, Suspended, Wing, Flying,
      Stand Up, Bobsled, Pipeline

Thrill Level: 😏 😃 😳 😵 😱

Height _____   Length _____

Speed _____   # of Inversions _____

Position: Front, Middle, Back

More About My Ride:

Roller Coaster Log

Date _____

Coaster Name _____

Location _____

Material: Steel or Wood   Year Opened _____

Designer _____

Type: Sit Down, Suspended, Wing, Flying,
        Stand Up, Bobsled, Pipeline

Thrill Level: 😒 😃 😳 🤯 😱

Height _____   Length _____

Speed _____   # of Inversions _____

Position: Front, Middle, Back

More About My Ride:

Roller Coaster Log

Date _____

Coaster Name _____

Location _____

Material: Steel or Wood   Year Opened _____

Designer _____

Type: Sit Down, Suspended, Wing, Flying,
      Stand Up, Bobsled, Pipeline

Thrill Level: 😏 😀 😳 🤯 🫨

Height _____   Length _____

Speed _____   # of Inversions _____

Position: Front, Middle, Back

More About My Ride:

Roller Coaster Log

Date _____

Coaster Name _____

Location _____

Material: Steel or Wood   Year Opened _____

Designer _____

Type: Sit Down, Suspended, Wing, Flying,
        Stand Up, Bobsled, Pipeline

Thrill Level: 😒 😃 😳 🤯 😱

Height _____   Length _____

Speed _____   # of Inversions _____

Position: Front, Middle, Back

More About My Ride:

Roller Coaster Log

Date _____

Coaster Name _____

Location _____

Material: Steel or Wood   Year Opened _____

Designer _____

Type: Sit Down, Suspended, Wing, Flying,
      Stand Up, Bobsled, Pipeline

Thrill Level: 😏   😃   😳   😲   😱

Height _____   Length _____

Speed _____   # of Inversions _____

Position: Front, Middle, Back

More About My Ride:

Roller Coaster Log

Date _____

Coaster Name _____

Location _____

Material: Steel or Wood   Year Opened _____

Designer _____

Type: Sit Down, Suspended, Wing, Flying,
      Stand Up, Bobsled, Pipeline

Thrill Level: 😪 😃 😳 😱 😨

Height _____   Length _____

Speed _____   # of Inversions _____

Position: Front, Middle, Back

More About My Ride:

Roller Coaster Log

Date _____

Coaster Name _____

Location _____

Material: Steel or Wood   Year Opened _____

Designer _____

Type: Sit Down, Suspended, Wing, Flying,
        Stand Up, Bobsled, Pipeline

Thrill Level: 😏 😃 😳 🤯 😱

Height _____   Length _____

Speed _____   # of Inversions _____

Position: Front, Middle, Back

More About My Ride:

Roller Coaster Log

Date _____

Coaster Name _____

Location _____

Material: Steel or Wood   Year Opened _____

Designer _____

Type: Sit Down, Suspended, Wing, Flying,
      Stand Up, Bobsled, Pipeline

Thrill Level: 😒 😃 😳 🤯 😱

Height _____   Length _____

Speed _____   # of Inversions _____

Position: Front, Middle, Back

More About My Ride:

Roller Coaster Log

Date _____

Coaster Name _____

Location _____

Material: Steel or Wood   Year Opened _____

Designer _____

Type: Sit Down, Suspended, Wing, Flying,
        Stand Up, Bobsled, Pipeline

Thrill Level: 😔 😃 😳 🤯 😱

Height _____   Length _____

Speed _____   # of Inversions _____

Position: Front, Middle, Back

More About My Ride:

Roller Coaster Log

Date _____

Coaster Name _____

Location _____

Material: Steel or Wood   Year Opened _____

Designer _____

Type: Sit Down, Suspended, Wing, Flying,
       Stand Up, Bobsled, Pipeline

Thrill Level: 😒 😃 😮 🤯 😱

Height _____   Length _____

Speed _____   # of Inversions _____

Position: Front, Middle, Back

More About My Ride:

Roller Coaster Log

Date _____

Coaster Name _____

Location _____

Material: Steel or Wood   Year Opened _____

Designer _____

Type: Sit Down, Suspended, Wing, Flying,
        Stand Up, Bobsled, Pipeline

Thrill Level: 😏 😃 😳 😲 😱

Height _____   Length _____

Speed _____   # of Inversions _____

Position: Front, Middle, Back

More About My Ride:

Roller Coaster Log

Date _____

Coaster Name _____

Location _____

Material: Steel or Wood   Year Opened _____

Designer _____

Type: Sit Down, Suspended, Wing, Flying,
      Stand Up, Bobsled, Pipeline

Thrill Level: 😌 😃 😳 😱 😨

Height _____   Length _____

Speed _____   # of Inversions _____

Position: Front, Middle, Back

More About My Ride:

Roller Coaster Log

Date _____

Coaster Name _____

Location _____

Material: Steel or Wood   Year Opened _____

Designer _____

Type: Sit Down, Suspended, Wing, Flying,
      Stand Up, Bobsled, Pipeline

Thrill Level: 😏 😃 😯 🤯 😱

Height _____   Length _____

Speed _____   # of Inversions _____

Position: Front, Middle, Back

More About My Ride:

Roller Coaster Log

Date _____

Coaster Name _____

Location _____

Material: Steel or Wood   Year Opened _____

Designer _____

Type: Sit Down, Suspended, Wing, Flying,
        Stand Up, Bobsled, Pipeline

Thrill Level: 😏   😃   😳   😱   😨

Height _____   Length _____

Speed _____   # of Inversions _____

Position: Front, Middle, Back

More About My Ride:

Roller Coaster Log

Date _____

Coaster Name _____

Location _____

Material: Steel or Wood   Year Opened _____

Designer _____

Type: Sit Down, Suspended, Wing, Flying,
        Stand Up, Bobsled, Pipeline

Thrill Level: 😒 😃 😳 😵 😱

Height _____   Length _____

Speed _____   # of Inversions _____

Position: Front, Middle, Back

More About My Ride:

Roller Coaster Log

Date _____

Coaster Name _____

Location _____

Material: Steel or Wood   Year Opened _____

Designer _____

Type: Sit Down, Suspended, Wing, Flying,
        Stand Up, Bobsled, Pipeline

Thrill Level: 😒 😄 😦 🤪 ⛄

Height _____   Length _____

Speed _____   # of Inversions _____

Position: Front, Middle, Back

More About My Ride:

Roller Coaster Log

Date _____

Coaster Name _____

Location _____

Material: Steel or Wood   Year Opened _____

Designer _____

Type: Sit Down, Suspended, Wing, Flying,
        Stand Up, Bobsled, Pipeline

Thrill Level: 😌 😃 😳 😲 ⓐ

Height _____   Length _____

Speed _____   # of Inversions _____

Position: Front, Middle, Back

More About My Ride:

Roller Coaster Log

Date _____

Coaster Name _____

Location _____

Material: Steel or Wood   Year Opened _____

Designer _____

Type: Sit Down, Suspended, Wing, Flying,
        Stand Up, Bobsled, Pipeline

Thrill Level: 😌 😃 😲 😵 😱

Height _____   Length _____

Speed _____   # of Inversions _____

Position: Front, Middle, Back

More About My Ride:

Roller Coaster Log

Date _____

Coaster Name _____

Location _____

Material: Steel or Wood   Year Opened _____

Designer _____

Type: Sit Down, Suspended, Wing, Flying,
      Stand Up, Bobsled, Pipeline

Thrill Level: 😏 😃 😳 🤯 😱

Height _____   Length _____

Speed _____   # of Inversions _____

Position: Front, Middle, Back

More About My Ride:

Roller Coaster Log

Date _____

Coaster Name _____

Location _____

Material: Steel or Wood   Year Opened _____

Designer _____

Type: Sit Down, Suspended, Wing, Flying,
         Stand Up, Bobsled, Pipeline

Thrill Level: 😌 😃 😯 🤯 😱

Height _____   Length _____

Speed _____   # of Inversions _____

Position: Front, Middle, Back

More About My Ride:

Roller Coaster Log

Date _____

Coaster Name _____

Location _____

Material: Steel or Wood   Year Opened _____

Designer _____

Type: Sit Down, Suspended, Wing, Flying,
          Stand Up, Bobsled, Pipeline

Thrill Level: 😏 😃 😲 🤯 😱

Height _____   Length _____

Speed _____   # of Inversions _____

Position: Front, Middle, Back

More About My Ride:

Roller Coaster Log

Date _____

Coaster Name _____

Location _____

Material: Steel or Wood   Year Opened _____

Designer _____

Type: Sit Down, Suspended, Wing, Flying,
        Stand Up, Bobsled, Pipeline

Thrill Level: 😔 😃 😳 🤯 😱

Height _____   Length _____

Speed _____   # of Inversions _____

Position: Front, Middle, Back

More About My Ride:

Roller Coaster Log

Date _____

Coaster Name _____

Location _____

Material: Steel or Wood   Year Opened _____

Designer _____

Type: Sit Down, Suspended, Wing, Flying,
         Stand Up, Bobsled, Pipeline

Thrill Level: 😌 😃 😳 😲 😱

Height _____   Length _____

Speed _____   # of Inversions _____

Position: Front, Middle, Back

More About My Ride:

Roller Coaster Log

Date _____

Coaster Name _____

Location _____

Material: Steel or Wood   Year Opened _____

Designer _____

Type: Sit Down, Suspended, Wing, Flying,
      Stand Up, Bobsled, Pipeline

Thrill Level: 😌 😃 😳 😱 ☹

Height _____   Length _____

Speed _____   # of Inversions _____

Position: Front, Middle, Back

More About My Ride:

Roller Coaster Log

Date _____

Coaster Name _____

Location _____

Material: Steel or Wood   Year Opened _____

Designer _____

Type: Sit Down, Suspended, Wing, Flying,
      Stand Up, Bobsled, Pipeline

Thrill Level: 😪 😃 😳 🤯 😱

Height _____   Length _____

Speed _____   # of Inversions _____

Position: Front, Middle, Back

More About My Ride:

Roller Coaster Log

Date _____

Coaster Name _____

Location _____

Material: Steel or Wood   Year Opened _____

Designer _____

Type: Sit Down, Suspended, Wing, Flying,
        Stand Up, Bobsled, Pipeline

Thrill Level: 😏   😃   😳   🤯   😱

Height _____   Length _____

Speed _____   # of Inversions _____

Position: Front, Middle, Back

More About My Ride:

Roller Coaster Log

Date _____

Coaster Name _____

Location _____

Material: Steel or Wood   Year Opened _____

Designer _____

Type: Sit Down, Suspended, Wing, Flying,
        Stand Up, Bobsled, Pipeline

Thrill Level: 😴 😃 😳 🤯 😱

Height _____   Length _____

Speed _____   # of Inversions _____

Position: Front, Middle, Back

More About My Ride:

Roller Coaster Log

Date _____

Coaster Name _____

Location _____

Material: Steel or Wood   Year Opened _____

Designer _____

Type: Sit Down, Suspended, Wing, Flying,
        Stand Up, Bobsled, Pipeline

Thrill Level: 😒 😃 😲 🤯 😱

Height _____   Length _____

Speed _____   # of Inversions _____

Position: Front, Middle, Back

More About My Ride:

Roller Coaster Log

Date _____

Coaster Name _____

Location _____

Material: Steel or Wood   Year Opened _____

Designer _____

Type: Sit Down, Suspended, Wing, Flying,
      Stand Up, Bobsled, Pipeline

Thrill Level: 😴   😃   😳   🤯   😱

Height _____   Length _____

Speed _____   # of Inversions _____

Position: Front, Middle, Back

More About My Ride:

Roller Coaster Log

Date _____

Coaster Name _____

Location _____

Material: Steel or Wood   Year Opened _____

Designer _____

Type: Sit Down, Suspended, Wing, Flying,
        Stand Up, Bobsled, Pipeline

Thrill Level: 😒 😃 😮 🤯 😱

Height _____   Length _____

Speed _____   # of Inversions _____

Position: Front, Middle, Back

More About My Ride:

Roller Coaster Log

Date _____

Coaster Name _____

Location _____

Material: Steel or Wood   Year Opened _____

Designer _____

Type: Sit Down, Suspended, Wing, Flying,
     Stand Up, Bobsled, Pipeline

Thrill Level: 😌 😃 😳 🤯 😱

Height _____   Length _____

Speed _____   # of Inversions _____

Position: Front, Middle, Back

More About My Ride:

Roller Coaster Log

Date _____

Coaster Name _____

Location _____

Material: Steel or Wood   Year Opened _____

Designer _____

Type: Sit Down, Suspended, Wing, Flying,
        Stand Up, Bobsled, Pipeline

Thrill Level: 😌 😃 😳 😵 😱

Height _____   Length _____

Speed _____   # of Inversions _____

Position: Front, Middle, Back

More About My Ride:

Roller Coaster Log

Date _____

Coaster Name _____

Location _____

Material: Steel or Wood   Year Opened _____

Designer _____

Type: Sit Down, Suspended, Wing, Flying,
       Stand Up, Bobsled, Pipeline

Thrill Level: 😏 😃 😲 🤯 😱

Height _____   Length _____

Speed _____   # of Inversions _____

Position: Front, Middle, Back

More About My Ride:

Roller Coaster Log

Date _____

Coaster Name _____

Location _____

Material: Steel or Wood   Year Opened _____

Designer _____

Type: Sit Down, Suspended, Wing, Flying,
      Stand Up, Bobsled, Pipeline

Thrill Level: 😒   😃   😳   🤯   😱

Height _____   Length _____

Speed _____   # of Inversions _____

Position: Front, Middle, Back

More About My Ride:

Roller Coaster Log

Date _____

Coaster Name _____

Location _____

Material: Steel or Wood   Year Opened _____

Designer _____

Type: Sit Down, Suspended, Wing, Flying,
        Stand Up, Bobsled, Pipeline

Thrill Level: 😏 😃 😳 😲 😱

Height _____   Length _____

Speed _____   # of Inversions _____

Position: Front, Middle, Back

More About My Ride:

Roller Coaster Log

Date _____

Coaster Name _____

Location _____

Material: Steel or Wood   Year Opened _____

Designer _____

Type: Sit Down, Suspended, Wing, Flying,
      Stand Up, Bobsled, Pipeline

Thrill Level: 😌 😃 😳 🤯 😱

Height _____   Length _____

Speed _____   # of Inversions _____

Position: Front, Middle, Back

More About My Ride:

Roller Coaster Log

Date _____

Coaster Name _____

Location _____

Material: Steel or Wood   Year Opened _____

Designer _____

Type: Sit Down, Suspended, Wing, Flying,
      Stand Up, Bobsled, Pipeline

Thrill Level: 😒 😀 😮 😲 😱

Height _____   Length _____

Speed _____   # of Inversions _____

Position: Front, Middle, Back

More About My Ride:

Roller Coaster Log

Date _____

Coaster Name _____

Location _____

Material: Steel or Wood   Year Opened _____

Designer _____

Type: Sit Down, Suspended, Wing, Flying,
      Stand Up, Bobsled, Pipeline

Thrill Level: 😒   😃   😳   😲   😱

Height _____   Length _____

Speed _____   # of Inversions _____

Position: Front, Middle, Back

More About My Ride:

Roller Coaster Log

Date _____

Coaster Name _____

Location _____

Material: Steel or Wood   Year Opened _____

Designer _____

Type: Sit Down, Suspended, Wing, Flying,
        Stand Up, Bobsled, Pipeline

Thrill Level: 😒   😃   😶   🤯   😱

Height _____   Length _____

Speed _____   # of Inversions _____

Position: Front, Middle, Back

More About My Ride:

Roller Coaster Log

Date _____

Coaster Name _____

Location _____

Material: Steel or Wood   Year Opened _____

Designer _____

Type: Sit Down, Suspended, Wing, Flying,
        Stand Up, Bobsled, Pipeline

Thrill Level: 😒 😃 😳 😲 😱

Height _____   Length _____

Speed _____   # of Inversions _____

Position: Front, Middle, Back

More About My Ride:

Roller Coaster Log

Date _____

Coaster Name _____

Location _____

Material: Steel or Wood   Year Opened _____

Designer _____

Type: Sit Down, Suspended, Wing, Flying,
      Stand Up, Bobsled, Pipeline

Thrill Level: 😏 😃 😳 🤪 😨

Height _____   Length _____

Speed _____   # of Inversions _____

Position: Front, Middle, Back

More About My Ride:

Roller Coaster Log

Date _____

Coaster Name _____

Location _____

Material: Steel or Wood   Year Opened _____

Designer _____

Type: Sit Down, Suspended, Wing, Flying,
      Stand Up, Bobsled, Pipeline

Thrill Level: 😌 😃 😳 😱 😨

Height _____   Length _____

Speed _____   # of Inversions _____

Position: Front, Middle, Back

More About My Ride:

Roller Coaster Log

Date _____

Coaster Name _____

Location _____

Material: Steel or Wood   Year Opened _____

Designer _____

Type: Sit Down, Suspended, Wing, Flying,
        Stand Up, Bobsled, Pipeline

Thrill Level: 😏 😃 😳 😮 😱

Height _____   Length _____

Speed _____   # of Inversions _____

Position: Front, Middle, Back

More About My Ride:

Roller Coaster Log

Date _____

Coaster Name _____

Location _____

Material: Steel or Wood   Year Opened _____

Designer _____

Type: Sit Down, Suspended, Wing, Flying,
          Stand Up, Bobsled, Pipeline

Thrill Level: 😏   😃   😲   🤯   😱

Height _____   Length _____

Speed _____   # of Inversions _____

Position: Front, Middle, Back

More About My Ride:

Roller Coaster Log

Date _____

Coaster Name _____

Location _____

Material: Steel or Wood   Year Opened _____

Designer _____

Type: Sit Down, Suspended, Wing, Flying,
     Stand Up, Bobsled, Pipeline

Thrill Level: 😌 😃 😳 🤯 😱

Height _____   Length _____

Speed _____   # of Inversions _____

Position: Front, Middle, Back

More About My Ride:

Roller Coaster Log

Date _____

Coaster Name _____

Location _____

Material: Steel or Wood   Year Opened _____

Designer _____

Type: Sit Down, Suspended, Wing, Flying,
         Stand Up, Bobsled, Pipeline

Thrill Level: 😏 😃 😳 🤯 😱

Height _____   Length _____

Speed _____   # of Inversions _____

Position: Front, Middle, Back

More About My Ride:

Roller Coaster Log

Date _____

Coaster Name _____

Location _____

Material: Steel or Wood   Year Opened _____

Designer _____

Type: Sit Down, Suspended, Wing, Flying,
        Stand Up, Bobsled, Pipeline

Thrill Level: 😌 😃 😳 😲 😱

Height _____   Length _____

Speed _____   # of Inversions _____

Position: Front, Middle, Back

More About My Ride:

Roller Coaster Log

Date _____

Coaster Name _____

Location _____

Material: Steel or Wood   Year Opened _____

Designer _____

Type: Sit Down, Suspended, Wing, Flying,
       Stand Up, Bobsled, Pipeline

Thrill Level: 😴 😃 😳 😵 😱

Height _____   Length _____

Speed _____   # of Inversions _____

Position: Front, Middle, Back

More About My Ride:

Roller Coaster Log

Date _____

Coaster Name _____

Location _____

Material: Steel or Wood   Year Opened _____

Designer _____

Type: Sit Down, Suspended, Wing, Flying,
         Stand Up, Bobsled, Pipeline

Thrill Level: 😏 😃 😳 🤯 😱

Height _____   Length _____

Speed _____   # of Inversions _____

Position: Front, Middle, Back

More About My Ride:

Roller Coaster Log

Date _____

Coaster Name _____

Location _____

Material: Steel or Wood   Year Opened _____

Designer _____

Type: Sit Down, Suspended, Wing, Flying,
        Stand Up, Bobsled, Pipeline

Thrill Level: 😒   😃   😳   🤯   😱

Height _____   Length _____

Speed _____   # of Inversions _____

Position: Front, Middle, Back

More About My Ride:

Roller Coaster Log

Date _____

Coaster Name _____

Location _____

Material: Steel or Wood   Year Opened _____

Designer _____

Type: Sit Down, Suspended, Wing, Flying,
       Stand Up, Bobsled, Pipeline

Thrill Level: 😏 😀 😳 🤯 😱

Height _____   Length _____

Speed _____   # of Inversions _____

Position: Front, Middle, Back

More About My Ride:

Roller Coaster Log

Date _____

Coaster Name _____

Location _____

Material: Steel or Wood   Year Opened _____

Designer _____

Type: Sit Down, Suspended, Wing, Flying,
       Stand Up, Bobsled, Pipeline

Thrill Level: 😌 😃 😳 😱 😨

Height _____   Length _____

Speed _____   # of Inversions _____

Position: Front, Middle, Back

More About My Ride:

Roller Coaster Log

Date _____

Coaster Name _____

Location _____

Material: Steel or Wood   Year Opened _____

Designer _____

Type: Sit Down, Suspended, Wing, Flying,
        Stand Up, Bobsled, Pipeline

Thrill Level: 😌 😃 😳 🤯 😱

Height _____   Length _____

Speed _____   # of Inversions _____

Position: Front, Middle, Back

More About My Ride:

Roller Coaster Log

Date _____

Coaster Name _____

Location _____

Material: Steel or Wood   Year Opened _____

Designer _____

Type: Sit Down, Suspended, Wing, Flying,
        Stand Up, Bobsled, Pipeline

Thrill Level: 😏 😃 😳 🤯 😱

Height _____   Length _____

Speed _____   # of Inversions _____

Position: Front, Middle, Back

More About My Ride:

Roller Coaster Log

Date _____

Coaster Name _____

Location _____

Material: Steel or Wood   Year Opened _____

Designer _____

Type: Sit Down, Suspended, Wing, Flying,
       Stand Up, Bobsled, Pipeline

Thrill Level: 😏 😀 😳 🤯 😱

Height _____   Length _____

Speed _____   # of Inversions _____

Position: Front, Middle, Back

More About My Ride:

Roller Coaster Log

Date _____

Coaster Name _____

Location _____

Material: Steel or Wood   Year Opened _____

Designer _____

Type: Sit Down, Suspended, Wing, Flying,
          Stand Up, Bobsled, Pipeline

Thrill Level: 😒 😃 😳 😲 😱

Height _____   Length _____

Speed _____   # of Inversions _____

Position: Front, Middle, Back

More About My Ride:

Roller Coaster Log

Date _____

Coaster Name _____

Location _____

Material: Steel or Wood   Year Opened _____

Designer _____

Type: Sit Down, Suspended, Wing, Flying,
        Stand Up, Bobsled, Pipeline

Thrill Level: 😏 😃 😳 🤯 😱

Height _____   Length _____

Speed _____   # of Inversions _____

Position: Front, Middle, Back

More About My Ride:

Roller Coaster Log

Date _____

Coaster Name _____

Location _____

Material: Steel or Wood   Year Opened _____

Designer _____

Type: Sit Down, Suspended, Wing, Flying,
        Stand Up, Bobsled, Pipeline

Thrill Level: 😏 😃 😳 😲 😱

Height _____   Length _____

Speed _____   # of Inversions _____

Position: Front, Middle, Back

More About My Ride:

Roller Coaster Log

Date _____

Coaster Name _____

Location _____

Material: Steel or Wood   Year Opened _____

Designer _____

Type: Sit Down, Suspended, Wing, Flying,
       Stand Up, Bobsled, Pipeline

Thrill Level: 😏   😃   😳   😱   😨

Height _____   Length _____

Speed _____   # of Inversions _____

Position: Front, Middle, Back

More About My Ride:

Roller Coaster Log

Date _____

Coaster Name _____

Location _____

Material: Steel or Wood   Year Opened _____

Designer _____

Type: Sit Down, Suspended, Wing, Flying,
      Stand Up, Bobsled, Pipeline

Thrill Level: 😏 🙂 😯 🤯 😱

Height _____   Length _____

Speed _____   # of Inversions _____

Position: Front, Middle, Back

More About My Ride:

Roller Coaster Log

Date _____

Coaster Name _____

Location _____

Material: Steel or Wood   Year Opened _____

Designer _____

Type: Sit Down, Suspended, Wing, Flying,
       Stand Up, Bobsled, Pipeline

Thrill Level: 😒 😃 😳 😵 😱

Height _____   Length _____

Speed _____   # of Inversions _____

Position: Front, Middle, Back

More About My Ride:

Roller Coaster Log

Date _____

Coaster Name _____

Location _____

Material: Steel or Wood   Year Opened _____

Designer _____

Type: Sit Down, Suspended, Wing, Flying,
      Stand Up, Bobsled, Pipeline

Thrill Level: 😒 😃 😳 😵 😱

Height _____   Length _____

Speed _____   # of Inversions _____

Position: Front, Middle, Back

More About My Ride:

Roller Coaster Log

Date _____

Coaster Name _____

Location _____

Material: Steel or Wood   Year Opened _____

Designer _____

Type: Sit Down, Suspended, Wing, Flying,
      Stand Up, Bobsled, Pipeline

Thrill Level: 😏 😃 😳 😱 🔔

Height _____   Length _____

Speed _____   # of Inversions _____

Position: Front, Middle, Back

More About My Ride:

Roller Coaster Log

Date _____

Coaster Name _____

Location _____

Material: Steel or Wood   Year Opened _____

Designer _____

Type: Sit Down, Suspended, Wing, Flying,
          Stand Up, Bobsled, Pipeline

Thrill Level: 😏 😃 😳 😱 😨

Height _____   Length _____

Speed _____   # of Inversions _____

Position: Front, Middle, Back

More About My Ride:

Roller Coaster Log

Date _____

Coaster Name _____

Location _____

Material: Steel or Wood   Year Opened _____

Designer _____

Type: Sit Down, Suspended, Wing, Flying,
      Stand Up, Bobsled, Pipeline

Thrill Level: 😏 😃 😳 🤪 😱

Height _____   Length _____

Speed _____   # of Inversions _____

Position: Front, Middle, Back

More About My Ride:

Roller Coaster Log

Date _____

Coaster Name _____

Location _____

Material: Steel or Wood   Year Opened _____

Designer _____

Type: Sit Down, Suspended, Wing, Flying,
          Stand Up, Bobsled, Pipeline

Thrill Level: 😴 😃 😳 😵 😱

Height _____   Length _____

Speed _____   # of Inversions _____

Position: Front, Middle, Back

More About My Ride:

Roller Coaster Log

Date _____

Coaster Name _____

Location _____

Material: Steel or Wood   Year Opened _____

Designer _____

Type: Sit Down, Suspended, Wing, Flying,
        Stand Up, Bobsled, Pipeline

Thrill Level: 😏 😃 😳 😱 😨

Height _____   Length _____

Speed _____   # of Inversions _____

Position: Front, Middle, Back

More About My Ride:

Roller Coaster Log

Date _____

Coaster Name _____

Location _____

Material: Steel or Wood   Year Opened _____

Designer _____

Type: Sit Down, Suspended, Wing, Flying,
        Stand Up, Bobsled, Pipeline

Thrill Level: 😏   😃   😯   😲   😱

Height _____   Length _____

Speed _____   # of Inversions _____

Position: Front, Middle, Back

More About My Ride:

Roller Coaster Log

Date _____

Coaster Name _____

Location _____

Material: Steel or Wood   Year Opened _____

Designer _____

Type: Sit Down, Suspended, Wing, Flying,
        Stand Up, Bobsled, Pipeline

Thrill Level: 😒 😃 😳 🤯 🔽

Height _____   Length _____

Speed _____   # of Inversions _____

Position: Front, Middle, Back

More About My Ride:

Roller Coaster Log

Date _____

Coaster Name _____

Location _____

Material: Steel or Wood   Year Opened _____

Designer _____

Type: Sit Down, Suspended, Wing, Flying,
        Stand Up, Bobsled, Pipeline

Thrill Level: 😌 😃 😳 😲 😱

Height _____   Length _____

Speed _____   # of Inversions _____

Position: Front, Middle, Back

More About My Ride:

Roller Coaster Log

Date _____

Coaster Name _____

Location _____

Material: Steel or Wood   Year Opened _____

Designer _____

Type: Sit Down, Suspended, Wing, Flying,
        Stand Up, Bobsled, Pipeline

Thrill Level: 😴 😃 😳 😲 😱

Height _____   Length _____

Speed _____   # of Inversions _____

Position: Front, Middle, Back

More About My Ride:

Roller Coaster Log

Date _____

Coaster Name _____

Location _____

Material: Steel or Wood   Year Opened _____

Designer _____

Type: Sit Down, Suspended, Wing, Flying,
      Stand Up, Bobsled, Pipeline

Thrill Level: 😒 😃 😳 😲 😱

Height _____   Length _____

Speed _____   # of Inversions _____

Position: Front, Middle, Back

More About My Ride:

Roller Coaster Log

Date _____

Coaster Name _____

Location _____

Material: Steel or Wood   Year Opened _____

Designer _____

Type: Sit Down, Suspended, Wing, Flying,
        Stand Up, Bobsled, Pipeline

Thrill Level: 😒 😃 😳 😲 😱

Height _____   Length _____

Speed _____   # of Inversions _____

Position: Front, Middle, Back

More About My Ride:

Roller Coaster Log

Date _____

Coaster Name _____

Location _____

Material: Steel or Wood   Year Opened _____

Designer _____

Type: Sit Down, Suspended, Wing, Flying,
        Stand Up, Bobsled, Pipeline

Thrill Level: 😒   😃   😳   😵   😨

Height _____   Length _____

Speed _____   # of Inversions _____

Position: Front, Middle, Back

More About My Ride:

Roller Coaster Log

Date _____

Coaster Name _____

Location _____

Material: Steel or Wood   Year Opened _____

Designer _____

Type: Sit Down, Suspended, Wing, Flying,
        Stand Up, Bobsled, Pipeline

Thrill Level: 😒 😃 😳 😱 🫢

Height _____   Length _____

Speed _____   # of Inversions _____

Position: Front, Middle, Back

More About My Ride:

Roller Coaster Log

Date _____

Coaster Name _____

Location _____

Material: Steel or Wood   Year Opened _____

Designer _____

Type: Sit Down, Suspended, Wing, Flying,
       Stand Up, Bobsled, Pipeline

Thrill Level: 😏 😀 😶 🙀 😱

Height _____   Length _____

Speed _____   # of Inversions _____

Position: Front, Middle, Back

More About My Ride:

Roller Coaster Log

Date _____

Coaster Name _____

Location _____

Material: Steel or Wood   Year Opened _____

Designer _____

Type: Sit Down, Suspended, Wing, Flying,
        Stand Up, Bobsled, Pipeline

Thrill Level: 😌 😃 😳 🤯 😱

Height _____   Length _____

Speed _____   # of Inversions _____

Position: Front, Middle, Back

More About My Ride:

Roller Coaster Log

Date _____

Coaster Name _____

Location _____

Material: Steel or Wood   Year Opened _____

Designer _____

Type: Sit Down, Suspended, Wing, Flying,
          Stand Up, Bobsled, Pipeline

Thrill Level: 😒 😃 😳 😲 😱

Height _____   Length _____

Speed _____   # of Inversions _____

Position: Front, Middle, Back

More About My Ride:

Roller Coaster Log

Date _____

Coaster Name _____

Location _____

Material: Steel or Wood   Year Opened _____

Designer _____

Type: Sit Down, Suspended, Wing, Flying,
      Stand Up, Bobsled, Pipeline

Thrill Level: 😏   😃   😳   😲   😱

Height _____   Length _____

Speed _____   # of Inversions _____

Position: Front, Middle, Back

More About My Ride:

Made in the USA
Las Vegas, NV
11 February 2022